LESSONS OF THE FUTURE

Thriving Today
by
Understanding
Tomorrow

**COLLEGES, UNIVERSITIES, CORPORATIONS,
& QUANTITY BUYERS**

Bulk purchase discounts on this book are available
for sales promotions, premiums, fund-raising, or
educational use. Special books or book excerpts
can also be created to fit specific needs.

Write or or e-mail for information on our discount
programs.

Dedication

*To my wife, Dani, and our amazing baby girl, Montana.
You have shown me the true meaning of success. I cherish you.
I love you.*

—Andrew Duggan

*To my mom, Shirley and my brother, Peter, whose support
throughout my life has helped me become the man I am today.*

—David J. Murcott

Coming in the

***Lessons of the Future* Series**

Lessons of the Future Entrepreneur

Lessons of the Future Technology

Lessons of the Future Relationship

Lessons of the Future Woman

Lessons of the Future Man

LESSONS OF THE FUTURE

Thriving Today

by

Understanding Tomorrow

Andrew Duggan
David J. Murcott

STS Publishing
La Jolla, California

ISBN: 0-9665329-0-2
Library of Congress Catalog Card Number: 98-86065

STS Publishing
5580 La Jolla Blvd., Suite 376
La Jolla, CA 92037

www.futurelessons.com
Cover Design by Laurie Dietter
Printed in the United States of America.

Table of Contents

The future never just happened.
It was created.

— *Will and Ariel Durant, Authors*
"Lessons of History"

Acknowledgments

We would like to thank all those who helped bring our dream to life. The production of our vision could not have been accomplished without the exceptional talents of Scott Roberts, Jeremy Leng, and Laurie Dietter. We offer a special thanks to all those who read the original manuscript and helped us produce a better book— we trust we did you justice.

Andrew would like to thank: Noel, Ivan, Damien, Shirley, Tony, Amanda and Carol—you have been with me in all my travels. My proud parents, Noel and Angela Duggan, for your unconditional support and belief in a "dreamer." The lads—Clive, Derek, Denis, Rob and Dave—you have no idea how much you mean to me.

In addition, Dave would like to thank: Eric Saperston, Paige O' Brien and Kathleen Kelly for taking me on an incredible Journey. Jack Canfield and Kim Kirberger of *Chicken Soup for the Soul* for giving me my start in professional writing. John Ernster, for his unending friendship, support and encouragement. Andrew, for making me stretch far beyond my comfort zone. All those who shared their time and resources while I was with the Journey Foundation, special thanks to OZ Nelson (former CEO of UPS), Bill Sessions (former Director of the FBI), Ann Richards (former Governor of Texas), Alan Duke (Sr. Vice President-Walt Disney Television) and Henry Winkler.

Foreword

If you woke up tomorrow and found yourself five to twenty-five years in the future, what would your life be like? Think about that for a moment. For many people, a painful and disappointing scenario appears. They look at the future and see unfulfilled dreams and unrealized potential. Or, they see uncertainty. They wonder if, over time, they would have ever summoned up enough courage to start that new business, or write that book, or begin the family they always wanted.

For a select few though, a smile breaks out as they think of how all their hard work and dedication will have paid off. Then, they start listing their accomplishments, and the smile grows.

Which of those categories best describes you? The fact that you've picked up this book indicates that you don't want to end up in the first group. But, are you really doing what it takes to be a part of the second? That's what *Lessons of the Future* is about. It is a simple story with a powerful message.

Success, in projects, careers, relationships or life, doesn't just happen. It comes as a result—a reward if you will—for those with the determination to earn it.

Your future has not yet been written, and that is fantastic news. If you are prepared to take it, an exciting journey awaits.

Introduction

When we first decided to write a book about the rapidly changing world in which we live, we endeavored to compile a comprehensive description about the role technology will play in the future of society.

We found this to be an exciting opportunity and longed for the day when our ideas would be "unveiled" to the world. We spent countless hours scouring available resources, developing avenues of analysis, projecting future trends and drawing practical conclusions.

As the book matured, however, we found ourselves back at the drawing board.

We realized that though our concepts were unique, our format was not. There are countless books available which project future trends—many are excellent, and many are dry as old toast.

While we were confident we could contribute meaningfully to the first collection, we believed even more strongly that something new was in order.

Our recipe was straightforward—keep it short, keep it interesting and impart practical lessons that can be employed immediately to make a difference in people's lives.

Simple, at least in concept. In practice, writing a brief story proved much more challenging than a detailed analysis. Nevertheless, we hope we have achieved our goal. You, the reader, will be the final judge.

Should you use the information in this book to help build the future you desire, our mission will have been a success.

We encourage you to share what you are about to learn with your family, friends and colleagues.

And, we wish you the very best for today as well as tomorrow.

Andrew Duggan

David J. Murcott

Who Should Use This Book

While we chose a story that unfolds around a business situation, we have defined a model for success that can be applied to virtually all areas of life.

We therefore encourage you to liberally use the lessons described within. We are confident in their ability to work equally well for organizations and global corporations, students, teachers, parents and individuals alike.

—CHAPTER 1—

Jason Abbott was an unhappy man. He had endured eight long years in pursuit of his MBA. He had diligently labored six more years in the workplace to make a name for himself. Now, his world was crumbling around him.

Three months ago, he was laid off by his company. He had been a productive employee, they told him. But times were changing and he didn't seem to be changing with them.

At one time, Jason held a very promising future.
He had been a successful project manager for a large
consulting firm.

Though he had seen new technology looming around
the corner, Jason felt he was too busy to invest time in
his own professional development.

Time wasn't something he lacked today.

He was taking a break from his rather unsuccessful job
search to blow off a little steam.

He sat on his motorcycle overlooking the city, shoulders slumped and head hung low. He thought of all the wasted energy and hard work he had put into his career.

He blamed the company for selling him out.

He blamed the clients for never being satisfied.

He blamed technology for moving ahead and leaving him behind.

He started his bike and made his way home. He could feel his blood start to boil. His frustration gave way to anger, which grew into rage.

Jason twisted the accelerator. Faster and faster he rode, as if by going fast enough he could leave his troubles behind.

He was too caught up in his misery to see the stoplight change. But it did, and with it, so did his life.

In less than a second there was a car, a collision and darkness.

He was somewhere between sleep and consciousness when the bright white lights above him came into focus. His body convulsed with pain.

He heard voices but couldn't understand them. The lights suddenly dimmed, blocked by a figure. The doctor examined his eyes. "Sir, can you hear me?" Jason merely nodded.

"You've just been in an accident. Can you talk?"

"Yes," he replied in a whisper.

"I'd like to ask you some questions."

They were routine questions, simple questions like: What is your name? Where do you live? What is the date?

When Jason answered the first two questions, the doctor simply acknowledged his response. It was his answer to the third question which gave her reason to worry.

After a brief pause, she said, "I have one more question for you, Mr. Abbott. Who is the current President of the United States?"

She was unable to hide her concern at his answer.

"Mr. Abbott, you have experienced a severe blow to the head, and there appears to be some tissue swelling near your brain. I'm afraid it has affected a portion of your memory."

She continued, "Now, I want you to try to relax. This will quite likely clear itself up as the swelling decreases. In the meantime, I'd like to keep you here for a while, so we can run a few tests."

As she started to turn away, Jason called out. "Doctor, what is the date today?"

He couldn't believe it when she told him it was twenty-five years later than he though it was.

Was she joking? Did I hear her correctly? Am I dreaming?
That must be it, dreaming, Jason thought as the medication sent him drifting back to sleep.

——CHAPTER 2——

Jason awoke to the sound of curtains being opened in his hospital room. He looked up to see an elderly man in a dark suit step away from the window.

"Oh, good morning, sir. Thank heavens you're alright." The unfamiliar figure bustled around the room and never seemed to stop talking. The TV was on, but the sound was muted.

"Bloody foolhardy things, those motorbikes. I don't know why you insist on riding them. Still, the doctor said it appears you escaped with only a concussion. A few days of rest and we'll have you out of here before you know it."

Jason just stared blankly. His mind reeled from the accident and the bizarre incident with the doctor and her reference to the date.

He still wasn't completely sure what had happened, and he had absolutely no idea who this stranger was.

"Perhaps I should be more careful next time," he told the man. Then he introduced himself. "By the way, my name is Jason."

The little man stopped abruptly. "Sir, don't you know who I am?"

"No," Jason responded, "Should I?"

"If you're playing a joke on me, sir, I wish you would stop. I don't find it at all amusing."

Now it was Jason's turn to pause. "I'm sorry, but I've never laid eyes on you before."

"Oh dear, I think I should send for the doctor." As the strange man turned away, Jason caught him by the sleeve.

"Wait!" he ordered. "I'm a little confused right now. What's going on here? I want you to tell me who you are."

The response shook any remnants of sleep from Jason's body. "Sir, my name is Martin. I'm your personal valet and have been for the past eleven years."

Jason closed his eyes tightly and wished it would all go away. But, when he looked again, the little man was still beside his bed.

If he was having a dream, it was the most unusual one he had ever experienced. If he wasn't … well … Jason didn't want to think about that possibility.

There was nothing he could do. He wanted to run, but he was in too much pain. He wanted to scream but couldn't find the voice.

So, for the time being, he decided to go along with whatever game fate was playing with him and do the only thing he could, ask more questions. "Let's start from the beginning. Who am I?"

"This is terrible," Martin fretted. "The doctor said your memory might be affected, but I certainly didn't expect anything so serious. I'm not certain I know how to handle this, sir."

"You can start by telling me everything you know about me. And stop calling me sir!" Jason said irritably.

"Very well. Your name is Jason Abbott, and you are the chairman and founder of *Invisionation*, one of the world's largest business conglomerates."

"You have a wife, a son and two daughters, who are rushing home from your villa in France." Martin paused and shook his head, "Are you honestly telling me you don't remember any of this?"

"Let me ask the questions," Jason said tersely.

"Very well, Mr. Abbott," the valet replied.

Just then, the image on television caught Jason by surprise. The man in the picture looked familiar, yet somehow different.

As he looked closer, Jason realized he was seeing himself, only older. He was not a man in his early thirties but rather his late fifties.

"Turn it up!" he shouted. "Please."

"... Wall Street reacted cautiously to the news that Jason Abbott, chairman of the *Invisionation* network, was involved in a traffic accident last night. As the market opened, *Invisionation* stock dropped nearly a point. It quickly rebounded when the company released a statement indicating that the chief executive was not seriously injured and was expected back in the very near future. In other news ..."

Jason watched in silence and in shock. He turned to his bedside table and lifted a silver water pitcher, peering at his own blurred reflection.

The eyes that stared back were older, the face a bit more lined. He put down the pitcher and examined his hands, noticing the unmistakable signs of age. Jason Abbott was no longer a young man.

His trance was broken when Martin spoke. "Mr. Abbott, there are members of the press outside the hospital. It would be dreadful if they gathered news of your condition. I'm going to speak to your doctor about ensuring confidentiality."

Jason was suddenly distracted, drawn away from the sound of Martin's voice. Something was calling him, or pulling him, he wasn't quite sure which. It was a distant but menacing feeling. It made him uncomfortable. It made him want to leave. Then, as quickly as it had come, it vanished.

"Martin, take me home," Jason ordered.

"But, the doctor has insisted you stay."

"I'm not asking you, I'm telling you. I want to leave now."

—CHAPTER 3—

The ride *home* was as strange as everything else in Jason's new life. He sat in the back of a stretch limousine which took him to a sprawling estate, his estate.

Bewildered, dazed and uncertain, he entered the palatial home. People he had never met greeted him as though they knew him.

All around him were signs of a life he didn't remember living. There were pictures on the wall of a family he didn't know and rooms full of possessions he had never owned.

Despite the unfamiliarity, there was a strange sensation that this was indeed real. Jason was slowly coming to terms with the idea that this could be his life.

He was still uneasy; but, he had to admit, he was also rather impressed. He had managed to build a life beyond his wildest dreams.

If only he could remember how.

If only he could remember why.

Jason was determined to answer the puzzling questions surrounding his good fortune.

He had never been a man of great ambition, or so he thought. And, it was clear that his surroundings had come as the result of more than just hard work.

So, what could have happened to change the course of his life?

He tried to conjure up the missing years in his mind but to no avail.

He looked through a myriad of photo albums and explored the house, its furnishings and his belongings. Nothing here held any memories.

Still, he did feel an odd sense of connection, as if he truly did belong. It was the pictures of the family that touched him the most. He looked at one of his son and saw so much of himself - it was startling.

Jason also saw pictures of himself with his wife and couldn't recall ever seeing two people who looked more in love. And, the girls ... well, they were quite simply the most beautiful children he had ever seen.

Try as he might, Jason could remember nothing of them or of his life over the past 25 years. *The picture he was holding slipped from his hand as a slight shock rippled through his body. The menacing feeling returned. It was closer this time and getting closer every second.*

Again, the presence quickly departed but not before leaving Jason a little bit weaker.

He tried to shake it off and blamed the sensation on the accident. He returned his attention to the pictures, and, before long, the incident was nearly forgotten.

After several hours of exploring his home, Jason began to get a sense of why he had created such an extraordinary quality of life. It must have had a lot to do with his family.

He had never seen himself look so happy, so content or so fulfilled as he looked in the pictures. He realized there was nothing that man wouldn't do for the family that had given him so much.

Unfortunately, none of this answered the question about *how* he had created such a life. But, he had a pretty good idea where to find what he was looking for. With that thought in mind, he asked Martin to take him to the office.

Though weak and weary from his ordeal, Jason was eager. He could only imagine the size and scope of the company that had made him such an incredibly wealthy man.

He envisioned the huge office building with hundreds, perhaps thousands of people scurrying about, doing ... well, doing whatever it was his company did.

So, when the limousine pulled into a small, albeit exclusive, office complex, Jason was less than impressed with what he saw. *Multinational conglomerate my* ... he muttered.

—CHAPTER 4—

From the back seat, he looked out the window at a sign in the shape of a pyramid.

It displayed a single word: *Invisionation.*

"Martin, this office seems a little small to be the headquarters of such a large organization. Do we have another complex somewhere else?" he asked hopefully.

"No, sir," Martin replied. "This is it."

Though it wasn't nearly as impressive as he'd expected, this was still Jason's company. He suddenly became quite nervous at the thought of going inside. What would he say? How should he act? What was he supposed to do?

"Martin, I don't feel very well. I might need you to help me get through this day. Will it look suspicious if you come in with me?" he asked the valet.

"I have never been in there before," Martin responded. "However, I do know most of the staff from the parties you have hosted at the estate. Given your accident, I shouldn't think there would be a problem."

"Then let's get going. My curiosity is killing me."

The two men walked inside, where a polite but rather imposing security guard greeted them.

"Good morning, Mr. Abbott," the guard said. "I'm a little surprised to see you here today. How are you feeling?"

"A little banged up, but I'll survive. Thanks for asking."

Once again, Jason found himself in unfamiliar surroundings being greeted by strangers who appeared to know him quite well.

One man in particular seemed to pay close attention to the pair. Martin told Jason it was Alan Palmer, the company's chief of operations.

"Jason," he said from across the room. "My God, you look terrible. What are you doing here? You should be at home resting."

"You know me, Alan. I never have been much for inactivity. I'm still a little shaken up though, so I thought I'd bring Martin in to give me a hand today."

"Of course," Alan responded. "How are you, Martin? It's good to see you."

"Very well, thank you, Mr. Palmer. It's a pleasure to see you again," replied the valet.

"Alan, I thought we'd give Martin a little tour of our operations. In all the years he's been with me, he's never actually seen what I do."

Of course, neither had Jason.

Alan nodded and led the men down a hallway and through a set of large double doors into a massive circular room. Jason's eyes popped at the sight of the most sophisticated telecommunications system he had ever seen.

There were at least fifty large-screen monitors hung from the ceiling and computer terminals circled the entire room.

Alan ushered his employer and the valet to a raised platform in the center. There were several large leather chairs surrounding a luxurious conference table.

As the men sat, Alan began. "This is Mission Central, Martin. From here, Mr. Abbott manages his entire network of global operations."

Alan continued, "Our mutual employer is nothing less than a genius." Jason tried to feign moderate interest, while inside he hung on every word.

"*Invisionation* has transcended locality. By capitalizing on the latest communication systems, Mr. Abbott has been able to project his influence to every corner of the world."

Whatever misgivings Jason had about the size of the company soon vanished. Alan got up and walked around the platform.

"*Invisionation* manages and distributes financial services, medical care, legal counsel, business news, educational information, entertainment and consumer goods for customers throughout the world. And we do it for a fraction of the cost of traditional methods."

He continued, "In short, Martin, Mr. Abbott has engineered a one-stop-shop for virtually everything a person or business could ever need."

Genuinely intrigued, Martin asked, "How did it all begin?"

"I think Mr. Abbott would be the best one to tell that story, but I'll give it my best shot. It started when intellect, vision and imagination collided to create *Invisionation*."

"It wasn't enough just to be smart anymore. You had to possess the foresight and creativity to increase, harness and effectively use your mental power. If you wanted to truly thrive, you had to continually invent new ways to provide value to society."

"You had to have the vision to know what people wanted, the imagination to create the products or services which filled those needs and the intellect to turn your ideas into reality."

And that is apparently what Jason had done.

Alan punched some buttons on a keyboard and a wall-sized television screen came to life. The screen split into four quadrants. Three of the quadrants showed doctors. The fourth showed a patient.

The four people on the screen were each in different parts of the world. Yet, they were all involved in the same operation. The doctors were performing robotic surgery on the patient, who was in another country.

"*Invisionation* enables these surgeons to operate on more patients than they ever could in the past," Alan stated. "The doctors you see here are among the best in the world, but they are no longer separated by such barriers as distance and language."

"We didn't create the robotic arms they use to perform the surgery, but we did provide the communications network which allows them to have absolute certainty that the slightest movement of their hands will be perfectly replicated thousands of miles away."

Alan pressed some more buttons on his keyboard. The screen became a full-sized image of a group of Asian teenagers.

Through a translation device, the three men could overhear and understand a research and development conference that was taking place on the other side of the world.

Alan spoke, "This group of young people is working to create new interactive entertainment programs for their peers."

"These kids and hundreds like them who work with us throughout the world will all become quite wealthy. They'll each receive a commission based on the number of people who access their programs through the *Invisionation* network."

"It's simply another example of using intellect, vision and imagination to create and provide value to a large market. We sponsor thousands of similar projects with lawyers, educators, business people and scientists every day."

"But I use the *Invisionation* network quite often," Martin said. "The amount I get charged is so insignificant. How does the company make any money?"

Alan was quick to respond. "That's an excellent question. Every time our network is accessed, the visitor is charged our standard micro-transaction fee of about 1/10 of a cent."

"Although it doesn't sound like much, the hundreds of millions of transactions we do every day really add up."

"Our strategic partners in cyberbanking handle all the charges and accounting. Our associates in hardware and software development build and maintain the systems. So, there is really minimal work for us to do in the actual process of operations."

Jason was absolutely amazed at what he saw and heard. An empire had been built and he was its founder. As he looked around him he nearly missed it when Martin asked, "So, if you have all these associates doing so much of the work, what is it that you do?"

"That is the simple genius of *Invisionation*. We constantly improve our efforts to discern what our customers want, and we create the best way to provide the products and services that fulfill their needs.

Develop the *vision* to know what people want,

the *imagination* to create the products or services
that meet those needs,

and the *intellect* to turn your ideas into reality.

—CHAPTER 5—

"Jason, we have a Board of Directors' meeting." Alan said. "Perhaps Martin could wait for you in the lounge."

"Very well," Jason said hesitantly. He was getting used to having Martin around and felt a bit vulnerable at the thought of being without his new friend.

As he and Alan proceeded to the conference room, Jason wished he hadn't dressed so casually. He had been to board meetings at his old job and remembered how stuffy and formal the affairs had been.

He was apprehensive about meeting his directors. Surely, they would see through his little ruse. How could he pretend to talk intelligently about the issues *Invisionation* was facing when he hardly knew the company?

Jason's body tingled. It was much closer this time and more threatening than before. It wasn't so much a feeling as it was a presence. Something was chasing him, and he had no idea how to outrun it. Jason knew it was only a matter of time before it caught him. His heart began to pound.

As the presence was nearly on top of him, it suddenly vanished. Whatever it was, it left Jason feeling incredibly weak and gave him the impression that time was against him.

"Are you ready?" Alan asked him.

"Hmm? Oh, yes," Jason muttered. When they walked in, Jason was surprised to see that the room was completely empty. "Where is everyone?"

"Where is who?" Alan questioned.

"You know Jason, I'm starting to get concerned. You really don't seem to be yourself today."

With that, he opened a panel on the table. At the press of a button, a mural covering one of the walls split in two. As the halves separated, a bank of TV screens lit up behind them.

Under every screen was a plaque, each one bearing the name of a location: Berlin, Buenos Aires, Jerusalem, Kuwait, London, Los Angeles, New York, Paris, Tokyo and Washington, D.C.

The 10 men and women on the screens represented *Invisionation's* Board of Directors. Jason was the Chairman and provided the tie-breaking vote in the event of controversy.

Alan served the Board in an advisory capacity and generally ran the meetings on Jason's behalf (which was quite a relief to Jason on this particular day).

The members each looked into their own monitors to
see Jason sitting at Alan's side. They had all heard of
his accident and expressed their concern.

After a flurry, of *Oh, dears* and *Are you sure you're
alrights?*, the meeting got underway. Alan presented
the minutes for approval and went through a list of old
business items.

Much to Jason's delight, everything proceeded without
incident. He had not been required to comment once
and was pleased just to listen and learn.

It was when they reached the first new business item that trouble started to brew. Alan began, "Our first item is the proposed alliance with the Holotech Group."

He continued, "We have all seen the reports, but I'll give a brief overview. Holotech has requested funding for a rather bold initiative."

Alan described the company's proposal to develop the technology that would transmit a lifelike holographic image over the *Invisionation* network, projecting it through a computer terminal into the room with a client.

The interactive hologram would serve as a personal account representative. Using an artificial intelligence database, the hologram would be able to comment on client preferences, recall ordering histories and even engage in conversation with the client about personal interests and his or her family.

"The upside potential is enormous," Alan continued. "Over the past decade, we have increased our speed in delivering products and services to mass markets across the globe. But, we paid the price by decreasing our ability to give each customer a sense of personal connection."

"Although everyone wants it cheaper, faster and better, they still want to know how important they are to us. This alliance with Holotech could raise the bar for everyone and create an entirely new era in customer service."

But, the news was not all good. "Despite the benefits, there is a substantial downside. This is an expensive project, and Holotech is a small company with limited resources. If any major setbacks or malfunctions are encountered, Holotech might not be strong enough to survive them."

Paris spoke up first. "I think it's too risky. These people are not tested on a level of such magnitude. How can we trust them? Besides, my sources indicate that no one else in the industry is even close to implementing such a notion."

"Which is exactly why we should jump on it," replied Los Angeles. "We have a unique opportunity to deliver an exciting new service to our clients. The market testing in the bid report indicates this would be a phenomenal success."

New York was the next to speak up, "I hate to be a stick in the mud, but I'm a little concerned as well. This would be an enormous burden on our system. If we were going to do it, I would certainly feel better using a larger firm or at least a better proven one."

Jason thought that made pretty good sense. Perhaps caution was in the company's best interest.

Just then Berlin launched into a rather persuasive tirade. "You should be ashamed of yourselves! Mr. Abbott would never have been able to build this organization if his thinking were so limited."

Jason shrank a little in his seat.

"Have you forgotten our core commitment to mastery and how Mr. Abbott used it to improve the company at every level?" he continued. "Always improving, always growing, a little here, a little there - never was there an end to the effort to get better. Are we as good as we can possibly be at serving our customer? Of course not! There is no such thing as too much investment when it comes to improvement. *Invisionation* is **not** about what we **can't** do, it's about what we **can't** afford **not** to do."

London agreed. "My opinionated colleague is absolutely correct. In any case, where would we find a large company that was willing to take such a risk? This is futurist-level thinking. Large companies simply don't operate like that any more."

"That's why there are so few of them left," said Buenos Aires.

The division was intense. The arguments in favor went something like this; "These guys have their fingers on the pulse of society." ... "Smaller companies can turn on a dime, and that's what we need." ... "We can't ever let up on our efforts to improve."

The opposing arguments favored a more careful approach; "Let's give it some time." ... "Wait for another developer." ... "Nobody is complaining about our service." ... "What we're doing now seems to be working just fine."

The discussion wasn't really going anywhere, so Alan called for a vote.

As Jason sat in silence, his worst fear came true. It was a tie. He had heard all the arguments, for and against, and they all seemed perfectly logical. He didn't know what to do.

If you had asked him yesterday, he would have voted on the side of caution and not thought twice about it. But, that was yesterday.

Since waking up in the hospital, nothing in his life was like yesterday. This company ... this life ... they weren't built by a cautious man. They were built by a visionary.

Alan interrupted his thoughts. "Well, Jason, what's it going to be?"

The decision was tough for Jason, but easy for the visionary.

"I vote in favor of the contract," he said.

The meeting continued smoothly. As it broke up, Jason couldn't help wondering if he had just made a brilliant business decision or a huge blunder.

All in all, he felt confident about supporting the proposal. But, it certainly was out of character for him to make such a decision.

He and Alan left the room and walked down the hall. He looked to his operations chief for support. "What were your impressions of the meeting, Alan?"

"In all honesty, I was quite disappointed in the members who opposed funding the project. The risks involved were significant but not disastrous. We can always help Holotech build the back-end support structure if they need it."

He continued, "I got the impression that some of the members were a little too comfortable with the status quo, which is crazy. We'll get eaten alive if we're not always trying to astonish our customers."

"Yes, I suppose you're right," Jason offered halfheartedly.

Alan looked at him and smiled, "Sounds like you're getting soft on me, Jason. Aren't you the one who always says, 'Good enough isn't good enough any more'?"

"Do I say that?" Jason quipped.

"If those board members have truly forgotten about our commitment to mastery and improvement, we should invite them to spend a day in our office."

"What do you think that would accomplish?"

"If they saw your professional development program in action, it might just jog their memories. Where else are they going to see a company paying employees to invest a full 1/3 of each day into improving their skills?"

Jason had a difficult time believing that this was his idea. It hardly seemed like the best way to run a business. If everybody was so busy learning, when was anybody busy working?

And what guarantee did he have that these people he trained wouldn't jump ship for a better opportunity? No, he didn't care for this practice at all.

"I have to hand it to you, Jason. When you first talked about this mastery concept, I was more than a little skeptical. I mean, it seemed like an awfully big risk. But, you were absolutely right."

"Since offering our employees the chance to develop their professional skills," he continued, "productivity has gone through the roof, morale has never been so high, and the new opportunities our employees bring us are worth their weight in gold."

"Yes, well, it's all quite logical really," Jason stuttered.

"We had better hurry. We have a strategic partner screening in a few minutes."

As they walked along, a shiver went down Jason's spine, *I do need to hurry.*

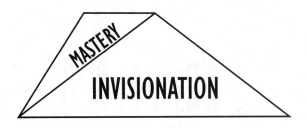

Develop a lifelong relentless pursuit of excellence.

Commit to daily incremental improvements in everything you do.

Outgrow your comfort zone.

——CHAPTER 6——

A lan and Jason reached an office, which bore the nameplate: *Jason Abbott, CEO. At last, my own office. Perhaps I can get some time to myself and make sense of this whole thing.*

Unfortunately, that would have to wait. The representative from the company wishing to join the *Invisionation* alliance was already there.

When Jason realized he was meant to run the meeting, he turned to Alan and made a quick excuse, "My head is really killing me, Alan. Can you lead this discussion?"

With a nod, the two men entered the room and greeted the woman who was waiting. Alan spoke. "Good afternoon, Ms. Yamoto. I'm Alan Palmer and I imagine you recognize Mr. Abbott."

"Of course I do," she replied with a sincere smile. "Gentlemen, it is an absolute pleasure to meet you both and quite an honor to be here today. Mr. Abbott, I hope you are recovering from your accident yesterday."

Managing a big smile, and an even bigger lie, Jason said, "I am indeed. Thank you."

He walked behind his desk and invited everyone to take a seat. As they did, Alan began to talk about *Invisionation's* alliances and strategic partnerships.

Ms. Yamoto listened attentively while Jason performed a cursory examination of his office. He casually picked up a business card from the holder on his desk and slipped it into his shirt pocket.

"*Invisionation*, Ms. Yamoto, is a company that has quite literally failed its way to success. Throughout our history, there have been countless events that nearly ended our existence."

Alan suddenly had Jason's undivided attention. "We have battled competitors who wanted us to falter, struggled with clients whose needs changed faster than we could respond and endured horrific shifts in the global economy that decimated other companies."

"Through it all, one thing, *and one thing only*, kept us alive."

Both Jason and Ms. Yamoto practically fell out of their chairs waiting for the golden secret of *Invisionation's* success.

"Alliances," Alan said. "Our ability to rely on and seek help from other committed visionaries enabled us to overcome every obstacle we faced."

Yet again, Jason found himself struggling with a core concept that had apparently made his company extremely successful. Asking other people for help wasn't exactly something he relished. He had always seen it as a display of weakness and rarely engaged in the practice himself.

Alan provided further explanation, "The simple truth is that life and business are about 75% struggle. As Mr. Abbott likes to point out, the struggle you're in might be new to you, but someone you know has already been through it."

"It seems silly not to use resources that would make your path easier. Unfortunately, most people choose to take on their problems alone. As a result, many businesses, relationships and lives end up in utter failure. Even those that do manage to stave off defeat will never reach their full potential, because they waste so much energy on the struggle."

I've never really looked at it like that before, Jason thought.

"Fortunately, said Alan, those are problems for the other guys. Our alliances keep us from having to go down that road. And, there are even greater benefits to building alliances that we haven't yet discussed."

"In addition to helping you survive through the tough times, alliances can be a powerful tool to help you thrive during the good times. *Invisionation* was founded on the idea that people and small organizations, working in unison can provide products and services more effectively and efficiently than large companies. This process has served us quite well throughout the years."

"In many ways, we operate much like the producers of a major motion picture. We bring together teams of talented people from a variety of fields to accomplish a common goal. We provide direction and support to the best of our ability. Then, we stay out of their way while they do what they do best, make magic."

He went on to describe how the majority of *Invisionation's* alliances were with individuals, people who had mastered their own skill sets and now contracted out their services, rather than gamble their careers on just one employer.

Alan described the very earliest *Invisionation* alliance, which was born when Jason created a project team of freelance contractors who underbid their former employer, a large consulting firm.

Jason couldn't help but smile at that bit of irony.

"Along the way, we encountered many different companies and individuals who, while extremely capable, didn't share one of our principal ideals. We fundamentally believe that giving back to the community is a necessity of modern business."

He continued, "Unfortunately, the success of *Invisionation* and other similar companies has come at a cost to society." Alan explained the effects of worldwide corporate downsizing and how millions of employees were displaced.

"Profiting in such an environment carries with it an obligation. Some of the companies in our alliance provide free job skills training; others fund school systems or relief agencies. How you choose to support your community is up to you. But, it must be a part of your organization's culture."

Ms. Yamoto's response was positive. Her family-owned company (an independent producer of business software) held the traditional cultural values of her country. They too felt tied to the wellbeing of their community.

The discussion moved comfortably to the next topic, that of integrity. "*Invisionation* does hold its partners to a high standard, Ms. Yamoto. But, again, the process has served us, our partners and our clients quite well."

"In this age of digital information and long distance business relationships, it's very easy to lose the personal touch, and with it the trust and accountability that are critical for any successful alliance."

"However," he continued, "we are committed to continuously improving the quality of our strategic relationships. We expect the same from our partners."

It was Ms. Yamoto's turn to speak. As she outlined her company's proposal, Jason and Alan were impressed, both by her vision and her character. An agreement was reached and the meeting soon came to a conclusion.

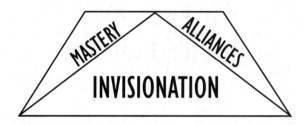

Ask for help from those who have already been where you are about to go.

Align yourself with talented people from a variety of fields to multiply your ability to deliver value to the marketplace.

Develop and nourish longlasting relationships with those who share your core values.

—CHAPTER 7—

Alan and Jason sat in the office and debriefed the meeting. *Without warning, the presence returned and hit Jason like a truck. He could almost feel a hot breath on the back of his neck.*

Alan looked at his boss. He was a wreck. His face was ghostly white, and he was soaked with sweat.

"There's no more time. I have to go," Jason gasped. "I have to go home." He didn't know why, but he knew that's where he had to go.

Alan tried to persuade Jason to return to the hospital, but the ailing man was determined.

The now familiar limousine pulled into the still unfamiliar driveway of Jason's estate. With what little strength he had left, he stepped from the car and made his way to the house.

When the door opened, two small girls came bounding from within.

"Daddy, Daddy," they gleefully squealed in unison. They both tried to tell him something but spoke so fast Jason couldn't understand. Each girl grabbed an arm as they vied for his attention.

Seconds later, a woman came out running. Though he had seen her pictures earlier in the day, Jason was at once struck by her beauty. Her name was Claire and she was his wife. She threw her arms around him and held on as if her life depended upon it.

"Oh, Jason," she cried. "Are you all right? Damn you and that stupid bike. I always knew this day would come again."

From behind her, a young man stepped forward. "Hey, Dad, you don't look so hot. How are you feeling?"

Jason was overwhelmed. He choked out a response. "I'll be fine. I swear." He couldn't understand why he felt the way he did. He had never met these people before. But, somehow, he knew deep inside, they really were his family.

In fact, it was the only certainty in this crazy new world of his. Since waking up from the accident, nothing had made sense. Not until now.

The money, the company, none of it was as important to him as his family, and Jason knew he would do anything for them. He hugged Claire and gently patted the girls' heads.

He looked at his son with a mixture of pride and regret. He was handsome, with a spark of intellect in his eyes.

But, Jason knew that for whatever reason, through whatever twist of fate, he had missed seeing the boy become a man, and it hurt.

They all went inside, and Jason asked them to tell him about their trip. In truth, he wasn't really interested in the details about France, he just wanted to hear the sound of their voices.

He had so much catching up to do. He looked and listened and learned about his family.

He had discovered in his earlier search of the house that Claire was a doctor, and his son, Scott, was a sophomore in college. The twins, Stephanie and Shannon, were entering fifth grade. They were so full of energy; Jason felt tired just watching them.

Apparently, he was going to join the family in a few days, but the accident had brought them home to him instead.

He marveled at how natural it felt to be with them. Jason looked at his wife of 25 minutes and felt 25 years worth of love.

They ate dinner and spent the evening together.
For the first time in his life, everything was right in
Jason's world.

Later, he and Claire sat in front of a roaring fire.
He leaned back into her arms and she gently stroked
his head.

Everything seemed clear to Jason. He had learned so
much in such a short time. He understood the tools
that had allowed him to build a successful life. More
importantly, he knew he could use them again.

He was absolutely certain about the purpose behind
his success. She was sitting next to him. Jason wanted
the best for his wife and children; nothing less would
ever do.

As he pondered these things, he realized he had
become the man he had seen in the pictures. He
was happy. He was content. He was fulfilled.

Jason could barely keep his eyes open when the presence returned for the last time. He almost didn't recognize it. It was softer, even comforting. He didn't try to fight it.

He could feel himself fading, and he didn't mind. He had found the answers to his questions and was surrounded by those who loved him. He wouldn't want it any other way.

As the darkness enveloped him, Jason surrendered.

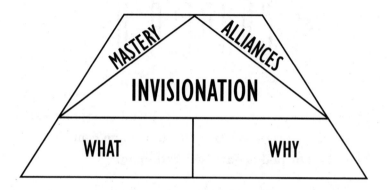

Know **what** you want and **why** you want it.

Define your objective and the steps you must take to reach your goal.

Develop a strong sense of purpose to stay focused on your path.

CHAPTER 8

He was somewhere between sleep and consciousness when the bright white lights above him came into focus. His body convulsed with pain.

He heard voices but couldn't understand them. The lights went dim, blocked by a figure. The doctor examined his eyes. "Sir, can you hear me?" she asked. "Is your name Jason Abbott? Jason, can you hear me?"

He nodded. The lights formed a halo around her head, and Jason was unable to see her face.

"Can you talk?"

His ears were ringing and the voice seemed distant.

"Yes," he replied in a whisper.

"You've been in an accident."

His mind began to whirl. "No ... No ... not again," he thought to himself. "What's happening to me?"

The doctor saw the fear in his eyes and put her hand gently on his shoulder.

"Relax, Mr. Abbott. You're going to be just fine, really. Would you like us to contact someone for you?"

Battered, bruised, confused and distraught, Jason called out for his wife, "Claire."

"Yes, my name is Claire," replied the doctor. "I asked you if there was anyone we could contact for you?"

The voice ... it wasn't possible. But, it was. He moved his head to avoid the lights and saw her standing above him.

It was Claire! It was really her! But, she looked so much younger than the woman he held last night. She looked like she had in the old pictures at the estate.

"Claire …Is it really you?"

"I'm sorry, Mr. Abbott, but I don't believe I know you," replied the puzzled physician. "In fact, when they brought you in, we weren't even sure who you were. I'm afraid you didn't have a wallet or any identification."

Jason couldn't stop his head from spinning. What could this mean?

Was yesterday just a dream after all?

Had he created the imaginary life with the imaginary wife after catching a glimpse of the doctor when they brought him to the hospital?

Was he truly a captain of industry, or was he still just an unemployed and unemployable project manager?

As reality set in, Jason's heart began to sink.

He looked up to see Claire staring at something in her hands.

"All you had in your pocket was this business card with your name on it," she said. "I tried to call the number, but it doesn't seem to exist. Tell me, Mr. Abbott, what is *Invisionation?* Is that your company?"

His pulse quickened as he took the card from her hand. As he laid eyes on the pyramid logo, an uncontrollable smile broke out across his face.

Jason had been to the future. And, it looked as though he had brought a little piece back with him.

He had no idea what magical things had recently transpired. In truth, he didn't really want to know. He understood that the mystery surrounding his life had worked for good, and he was grateful.

He leaned back to rest, knowing he had his work cut out for him.

Jason Abbott was about to make the future repeat itself.

He smiled at the woman who would one day be his
wife and the mother of his children.

"Well, Claire, … may I call you Claire?" he asked.
"*Invisionation* began when intellect, vision and
imagination collided…"

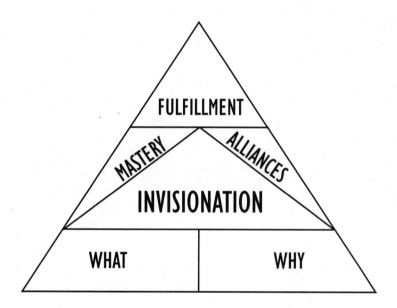

THE END

Hungry for More?

LESSONS OF THE FUTURE
GUIDEBOOK

Use this practical step-by-step guide to:

- Discover your mission.

- Determine your driving force.

- Unleash the awesome potential of your mind.

- Embark on a lifelong journey of never-ending improvement.

- Surround yourself with a network of people who can help fulfill your mission.

- Build the life you desire ... the life you deserve.

Three ways to order:

Call: 1-888-826-6577

Visit: www.futurelessons.com

Write: STS Publishing
5580 La Jolla Blvd., Suite 376
La Jolla, CA 92037

$15.95 plus $3.95 shipping and handling

IN SUMMARY

ABOUT THE SYMBOL

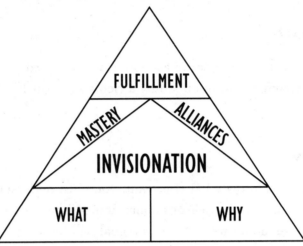

One of the greatest challenges of our time *is* time. The demands we place on ourselves in this hustle and bustle world are nothing short of tremendous. With all the stress and strain of *everyday life*, we seem to forget that *every day of life* is a precious gift.

Through the *Invisionation* symbol, we have endeavored to encapsulate the core ideas that make life the rewarding adventure it was meant to be. Individually, these ideas are not new. In fact, they have been around since the dawn of mankind.

But, used together, they can unlock one of the most powerful forces in the universe, the potential of the human mind.

It is our great pleasure to present to you the *Lessons of the Future.*

What?

Know what you want to accomplish. A directed mind is a key component to obtaining a rich and rewarding life.

Why?

Once you know what you want, you must understand why you want it. Reasons come first. Without a strong purpose, no desire, no plan, no goal will be achieved.

Successfully answering these two questions forms the foundation upon which any achievement can be built, whether you are endeavoring to complete a project, accomplish a goal or create an extraordinary quality of life.

Invisionation

Intellect, vision and imagination - use the immeasurable power of your mind to produce that which you desire. All creation comes from an idea. Harness this force to your advantage.

Mastery

Life is about consistent growth and improvement. Mastery is about your commitment to the process.

Daily, incremental improvements—in all areas of your life—will yield returns beyond your wildest expectations.

Alliances

By continually seeking out new people and organizations to help you accomplish your mission, you will increase your ability to influence the world around you.

And, always remember, nothing great was ever *truly* achieved alone. Any result accomplished in a vacuum quickly loses its ability to make us happy. It is in sharing our successes and failures with a community of colleagues, family and friends that joy is born.

Work with people who share your vision of the world, to build the world of your dreams.

Fulfillment

Live with a strong sense of purpose; use your mind to create the life you desire; constantly improve your ability to deliver value to society; align yourself with people to amplify your experiences.

It is after combining and applying the previous lessons that we come to fulfillment. Did we meet our goals and objectives? Can we improve upon our process?

Fulfillment is the retrospective view we take to examine the path that we're on and prepare ourselves for the journey that lies ahead.

The Lessons

Use this symbol to remind you of these lessons. No matter your situation in life, good or bad, we salute you for having the desire to improve it. And we challenge you to make your life a masterpiece!

**Use These Lessons to Build
the Life You Desire.**

**Share These Lessons and
Build a Life of Fulfillment.**

Our Mission

The world around us is changing incredibly fast. Unfortunately, like the character in *Lessons of the Future*, many people are not changing with it.

Now, more than ever, a commitment to constant learning and consistent improvement is vital for success in any project, career, relationship or life.

The future will not look kindly on those who fail to grasp that simple lesson.

Our Purpose: To equip people with the tools they need to build a better future.

Our Mission: To develop and deliver entertaining, enlightening and empowering performance systems that unleash potential, promote achievement and inspire significance.

Our Vision: A world made better by people working together to create opportunity for themselves and each other.

About the Authors

Andrew Duggan is a respected authority on technology and its impact on society, the workplace and the global economy.

An international management consultant, he advises his clients on business strategies and global business trends, positioning them for success in the 21st century.

Mr. Duggan has advised multinational corporations and governments including Delta Airlines, Pacific Bell, BP Oil UK, IBM, the Commonwealth Bank of Australia and the Singapore Government.

He lives with his family in San Diego, California.

About the Authors

David J. Murcott offers unique experience in preparing people for the marketplace of the future. As former Vice President of a research foundation, he worked to gather the collective wisdom of today's most accomplished business and political leaders.

He has discussed and evaluated success factors, market directions and employment trends with chief executives from such companies as Home Depot, Holiday Inn Worldwide and United Parcel Service.

Mr. Murcott is also a contributing author and editor of the #1 New York Times Best-selling book series, *Chicken Soup for the Soul.*

How to contact the Authors

We are excited about the interest in our story and we encourage you to share with us how your life was impacted. After all, that is our purpose.

With your permission, we would like to share your story with our expanding community.

Please send all correspondence to:

STS Publishing
5580 La Jolla Blvd., Suite 376
La Jolla, CA 92037

Or visit us at **www.futurelessons.com**

Andrew Duggan

David J. Murcott

Lessons of the Future World Wide Community

Visit our global community on the
World Wide Web

www.futurelessons.com

- Share in our online discussions and connect with a worldwide community of peers

- Give us your opinions, stories, and recommendations

- Contact the authors directly

- Preview other material from the authors

- Order Lessons of the Future products

- And much more....

Three ways to order more copies of

LESSONS OF THE FUTURE

Thriving Today
by
Understanding Tomorrow

Call: 1-888-826-6577

Visit: www.futurelessons.com

Write: STS Publishing
5580 La Jolla Blvd., Suite 376
La Jolla, CA 92037

$9.95 plus $3.95 shipping and handling.

If you are ordering multiple copies, please
add $1.00 for each additional item.

Future Watch Newsletter

The authors publish *Future Watch*, a monthly newsletter designed to help readers understand, prepare for and benefit from the latest trends in business and technology.

The newsletter includes articles, interviews with corporate, community and political leaders and interesting and informative stories gathered from our readers and research associates throughout the world. These articles entertain, enlighten, educate and provide new tools for succeeding in the global economy.

Three ways to subscribe to "Future Watch"

Call: 1-888-826 6577

Visit: www.futurelessons.com

Write: STS Publishing
5580 La Jolla Blvd., Suite 376
La Jolla, CA 92037

One year subscription is only $19.95

Notes

Notes